Rigby PM Benchmark
Kit 2
Teacher's Notes

Elsie Nelley and Annette Smith

Rigby PM Benchmark Kit 2 Teacher's Notes

U.S. edition © 2002 Rigby
a division of Reed Elsevier Inc.
1000 Hart Road
Barrington, IL 60010-2627
www.rigby.com

Text © 2002 Elsie Nelley and Annette Smith
Originally published in Australia by Nelson Thomson Learning

All rights reserved. No part of this publication may be reproduced or transmitted in any form or by any means, electronic or mechanical, including photocopying, recording, taping, or any information storage and retrieval system, without permission in writing from the publisher.

Permission is hereby granted to reproduce the Reading Records and Assessment Records on pages 20–82 of this publication in complete pages, with the copyright notice, for classroom use and not for resale by any teacher using the related student materials.

07 06 05 04 03 02
10 9 8 7 6 5 4 3 2 1

Printed in China

ISBN 0-7578-2133-2

Acknowledgements:
Cover and text photographs in *Teachers' Notes* by Lindsay Edwards and Bill Thomas
Cover photograph in *Trees on Our Planet* by Tasmanian Photo Library/Rob Burnett.
Text photograph by Tasmanian Photo Library/Steve Lovegrove.
Cover photograph in *Beavers* by Bruce Coleman Inc./John Swedberg.
Text illustration by Julian Bruère.
Cover photograph in *Cyclone Tracy Destroys Darwin* by Newspix.
Text photograph by Australian Picture Library/Corbis/Bettmann.

> The authors and publisher would like to thank the staff and students of the following schools for their assistance in testing the benchmark texts:
> Frankton Primary School, Hamilton, New Zealand
> Pukete Primary School, Hamilton, New Zealand
> Horsham Downs Primary School, Hamilton, New Zealand

> The authors and publisher acknowledge the assistance of the curator of the Susan Price Collection of children's books, National Library of New Zealand.

Contents

Introducing the *Rigby PM Benchmark Kit 2*	*5*
Reading Levels in the *Rigby PM Benchmark Kit 2*	*7*
Concepts	*7*
High frequency words	*7*
Sentence constructions	*7*
Meaning and logic	*8*
Reliability check for upper levels	*8*
Testing of benchmark levels	*8*
Matching kit levels to PM books	*8*
Guidelines for Taking the Assessment Record	*10*
The *Rigby PM Benchmark Kit 2* Assessment Procedures	*12*
Retelling	*12*
Reading records	*12*
Taking a reading record	*12*
Useful conventions for taking reading records	*13*
Identifying a student's reading level	*14*
Questions	*15*
***Rigby PM Benchmark Kit 2* Reading and Assessment Records**	*17*
Notes on running words	*17*
Example of a Completed Reading Record Sheet	*18*
Example of a Completed Assessment Record Sheet	*19*
Reading Record and Assessment Record Pro Formas	*20 – 79*
Example of a Completed Reading Progress Sheet	*80*
Reading Progress Pro Forma	*81*
Reading Record Pro Forma	*82*
Accuracy Level Charts	*83*

Introducing the *PM Benchmark Kit 2*

The *Rigby PM Benchmark Kit* is a comprehensive reading assessment resource:

- Teachers can use the *Rigby PM Benchmark Kit* to assess students' reading abilities using unseen, meaningful texts.
- The *Rigby PM Benchmark Kit* includes 30 accurately leveled texts ranging progressively from emergent level through fluency (grades K-5).
- Guidelines on how to administer the texts and interpret assessment data are on pages 10–15 of these teacher's notes.
- Each benchmark text has a prepared Reading Record and Assessment Record pro forma.

The *Rigby PM Benchmark Kit* offers to schools:

- a quality assessment resource
- a system for accurate identification of students' reading levels
- evidence of students' achievement and progress
- a vehicle for consistent assessment practices within and between schools
- data for school review and community feedback

Information can be used for:

- providing students with constructive feedback
- organizing students into groups of similar learning needs
- planning programs
- reporting to parents/caregivers
- transferring information within and between schools
- developing school policies for literacy learning
- presenting data for class or school accountability
- purchasing resources

Information gained from administering texts
in the *Rigby PM Benchmark Kit* can be collated as:

- an individual profile
- a class profile
or • a school-wide profile.

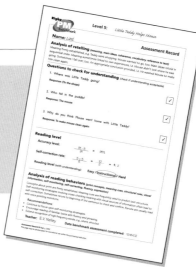

It is recommended that the *PM Benchmark Kit* be used **only** for assessment.

By using unfamiliar texts for assessment, the child's willingness to take risks, and ability to use and to integrate strategies independently can be measured.

It is important that teachers become familiar with the *PM Benchmark Kit* texts and procedures before administering the resource.

The student reads from the original text, not from the Reading Record sheet.

The *PM Benchmark Kit* will identify the student's:

- instructional reading level
- ability to read for meaning
- integration of meaning with structural and visual cues
- self-monitoring systems
- knowledge of print conventions
- rate of learning
- level of independence

Reading Levels in the *Rigby PM Benchmark Kit 2*

The reading levels of the *Rigby PM Benchmark Kit* texts have been achieved by careful consideration of the following factors:

Concepts

The situations and themes in the *Rigby PM Benchmark Kit* are relevant to students' ages, stages of development, and their likely experience of the world. Experience varies greatly, so concepts can never be perfectly matched to all students.

High frequency words

In the early level Rigby PM Benchmark texts, high-frequency words are introduced in the same order as in the Rigby PM Books. A very strict control over the number of high-frequency words and their order of introduction ensures that each Rigby PM Benchmark text matches a particular Rigby PM reading level. (See "Matching Kit levels to PM books" on pages 8 and 9.) This control allows children to read with 95% accuracy. At least 19 words in every 20 have been met before.

Most high-frequency words in Rigby PM books and PM Benchmark texts have been selected from those used most frequently in the free writing of young children. Other high-frequency words are those which storytellers need.

Sentence constructions

The sentence constructions are short and simple in the early Rigby PM Benchmark texts, and longer and more complicated as children's ability to understand language grows. Sentence constructions are partly influenced by vocabulary: when conjunctions and relative pronouns **because**, **when**, **who**, **which**, **as**, **if**, and **although** are introduced, sentences become more complex.

Level 2: *At the zoo*

Level 8: *My big sister*

Level 17: *The Greedy Dog and the Bone*

Level 30: *Black Beauty Encounters a Steam Train*

Meaning and logic

Each *Rigby PM Benchmark Kit* text has been written with a logical sequence of ideas driving the narrative. This helps young readers derive meaning from the text and thus come to an understanding of the purposes of reading. This focus on logic and meaning makes Rigby PM Benchmark texts useful tools for the analysis of children's reading behaviors.

Pages 2–3 *Baby Bear and the big fish (Level 7)*
Introduces the characters.

Pages 6–7 *Baby Bear and the big fish*
Introduces the problem.

Pages 12–13 *Baby Bear and the big fish*
Tension increases as problems mount.

Page 16 *Baby Bear and the big fish*
Happy ending for characters.

Reliability check for upper levels

The Fry Readability Formula[1] rests on the truth that short sentences are usually easier to read than long sentences, and that one-syllable words are usually easier to read and understand than multi-syllable words. Fry Readability is one of the checks used in framing stories and selecting extracts for the *Rigby PM Benchmark Kit* from levels 15–30.

Testing of benchmark levels

Each Benchmark text has been tested with children of an appropriate reading age to guarantee the suitability and readability of the text for a particular level.

Matching kit levels to PM books

Use the chart on the following page to match the PM Benchmark Kit level with the appropriate PM Collection (daisy) level, the PM Plus level, and the color level. The school grade levels are suggestions and teachers are encouraged to freely adjust these grade levels according to their personal evaluations.

---

[1] Edward Fry, *Reading Instruction for Classroom and Clinic*, McGraw Hill, 1972.

Grade Level	PM Benchmark Kit Level	PM Collection Level	PM Plus Level	Color Levels
K (Readiness)	1 2	1 2	1 2	Starters
Grade 1 (Pre-primer)	3 4 5	3 4 5	3 4 5	Red
Grade 1 (Pre-primer)	6 7 8	6 7 8	6 7 8	Yellow
Grade 1 (Primer)	9 10 11	11 10 9	9 10 11	Blue
Grade 1	12 13 14	14 13 12	12 13 14	Green
Grade 1 (Late)	15 16	15 16	15 16	Orange
Grade 2 (Early)	17 18	17 18	17 18	Turquoise
Grade 2	19 20	20 19	19 20	Purple
Grade 2	21 22	22 21	21 22	Gold
Grade 3	23 24	23 24	23 24	Silver
Grade 4	25 26	25 26	25 26	Emerald
	27 28	27 28	27 28	Ruby
Grade 5	29 30	29 30	29 30	Sapphire

Guidelines for Taking the Assessment Record

Follow these guidelines to place a student within the PM program

1. **Identify an appropriate starting level** for the student. Use previous records or your best judgement to identify a starting level.

2. **Sit at a table or desk**, in a quiet area where you will not be disturbed. The student should sit or stand beside you with the book.

3. **Record the student's name, age, and the date**, on the reading record sheet. Help the student to feel comfortable. Explain what you are going to do and why.

4. **Introduce the selected text by reading the title and discussing the cover.** The content of the story must not be expanded upon during this introduction. You can say:

   This story is about _____ and the names of the people in it are ___, ___ and___.

   Or you can read the introduction sentence provided above the text copy on the reading record.

   For students reading from levels 1–8 say:

   I'd like you to look at the pictures and read the words as much as you can to yourself. Then tell me about the story.

   For students reading from levels 9–30 say:

   I'd like you to read the story to yourself, then tell me about it.

   If the student asks for assistance while reading the text, say:

   First read the story to yourself, then you can tell me about it.

5. **When the student has completed reading the text,** say:

   Tell me what happened in the story (or book).

   Turn the reading record sheet over and analyze the student's retelling.

   If the student shows an in-depth understanding of the text, do not take a reading record. Instead, repeat the above procedures with the text at the next level.

   If the student is unable to retell the story, even with some teacher prompts, repeat the above procedures with the text at the level below.

6. If the above **evidence indicates** that this is the **correct reading level for the student**, proceed with the read aloud. Turn the Reading Record sheet back to the copy of the text and say:

   Now, I would like you to read the story (or text) to me.

   Record what the student says and does on the Reading Record sheet. (Refer to the completed example on page 18.)

7. **Ask the student the questions on the Assessment Record.** Check the box if the student's answer matches the one provided. Record alternate responses. Identify the depth of meaning that the student has gained from reading the text.

8. **Use the accuracy level charts on pages 83-86 to identify the student's accuracy level** and then calculate the self-correction rate. If the accuracy level is between 90%–95%, and the student has replied to the questions with appropriate understanding, the student's instructional reading level has been identified.

9. If the student reads **with greater than 95% accuracy** and replies correctly to all of the questions, **repeat the above procedures with the text at the next level**. If the student reads with **less than 90% accuracy**, repeat the above procedures **with the text at the level below**.

10. **Repeat steps 5–9 until the student's reading level is identified**. Then analyze the student's reading behaviors (refer to p. 15) and write the summary on the Assessment Record. Teaching objectives can be set from this information.

When is a student ready to move to the next level?

It is recommended that another benchmark assessment be taken after the student has read most of the PM books at the identified placement level.

The benchmark assessment will give a clear indication of the student's control of vocabulary, sentence structures, concepts, and use of skills and strategies to gain a depth of understanding.

For example, when a student is near the end of level 16 he or she has read many books, both fiction and nonfiction, in guided reading lessons. The student will have re-read many of them for pleasure.

If the student is tested on Benchmark level 16, and achieves more than 95% accuracy, and shows that he or she is reading with understanding, then the student is ready to move on to level 17.

The *Rigby PM Benchmark Kit* 2
Assessment Procedures

There are three key elements of the assessment procedure:

| Retelling | Reading records | Questions |

Retelling

Students reading from Benchmarks 1–8 are encouraged to retell the events after studying the illustrations and reading silently to the best of their ability. Students reading from Benchmarks 9–30 are asked to first read the text silently for the purpose of retelling it.

By having students retell what they have just read silently or interpreted from the illustrations, an assessment can be made of how well they have understood the text. The retelling should occur before the student reads the text aloud. The teacher's role is to identify the students' levels of understanding as they:

- demonstrate meaning
- recall the main ideas
- structure and organize the retelling
- retell with appropriate vocabulary and intonation.

During this task, the teacher remains a neutral observer while recording an analysis of the retelling on the assessment record. Only minimal prompting from the teacher should occur, such as "Did anything else happen?"

Reading records

> "Taking running records of children's reading behavior requires time and practice, but the results are well worth the effort. Once learned, the running record is a quick, practical, and highly informative tool. It becomes an integral part of teaching, not only for documenting children's reading behaviors for later analysis and reflection but sharpening the teacher's observational power and understanding of the reading process."
>
> *Guided Reading*, Irene C. Fountas and Guy Su Pinnell, Heinemann, 1996.

For a detailed description of taking, scoring, and analyzing reading records, see *An Observation Survey of Early Literacy Achievement*, Marie Clay, Heinemann, 1993.

Taking a reading record

- The student sits or stands beside the teacher.
- The text must be seen clearly by the student and the teacher.
- The teacher does not prompt and remains objective throughout the reading.
- It is suggested that up to 100 running words will provide adequate information for levels 1–10, 150 running words for levels 11-20, and up to 200 running words for levels 21–30.
- Recording should be done on a standardized record sheet. The *Rigby PM Benchmark Kit* provides an exact pro forma for every text.

Useful conventions for taking reading records

- Mark every word read correctly by the student with a check mark.

    ✓   ✓   ✓   ✓   ✓   ✓
    Mouse said, "Little Teddy! Little Teddy!"

- Record all attempts and errors by showing the student's responses above the text.

    Child: is | see
    ──────────────|──────
    Text: said |

- If the student self-corrects an error, record it as a self-correction, not an error.

    Child: is | SC
    ──────────────|──────
    Text: said |

- If a word is left out or there is no response, record it as a dash and call it an error.

    Child: —
    ─────────────
    Text: went

- If a word inserted, record it and call it an error:

    Child:
                                      now
              ✓   ✓   ✓   ✓   ^
    Text: Where are you going?

- If the student is told a word by the teacher, record it with a **T** and call it an error.

    Child: is |
    ──────────────|──────
    Text: said | T

- If the student appeals for a word, say "You try it." If unable to continue, record **A** for appeal, tell the student the word, and call it an error.

    Child: is | see | A |
    ──────────────|─────|───|
    Text: said | | T |

- Repetition is not counted as an error, but is shown by an **R** above the word that is repeated, as well as the number of repetitions, if more than one:

         R   R³
         ✓   or   ✓

- Record **R** for repeats plus an arrow if the student goes back over several words or even back to the beginning of the page:

    ┌──────────────────┐
    │   R
    ↓ ✓   ✓   ✓   ✓
    Where are you going?

- If the student appears confused, help by saying "Try that again." This is counted as one error only before that piece of text is reread:

    Child: ⎡ Get the dog   ⎤
            ⎢ ─── ─── ───   ✓ ⎥ TTA
    Text: ⎣ Go   to   bed,   Sam ⎦

Identifying a student's reading level

> The information on a Reading Record identifies the cues and strategies that a student uses while processing print. Reading levels can be identified when accuracy and self-correction rates are calculated. When a student successfully searches for extra information to correct an incorrect response, this is recorded as a self-correction.

- Put a **1** in the first two columns of the Reading Record sheet beside every error and self-correction. Count the number of errors and self-corrections and record these at the bottom of the first two columns.

- The accuracy rate is calculated by subtracting the number of errors from the running word count and dividing that number by the running word count. This accuracy rate has already been calculated for the first 15-30 errors for each benchmark text level and appears in the charts on pages 83-86.

Accuracy rate formula: $\dfrac{RW - E}{RW}$ = % of Accuracy

For example, if the running word count is 133 and the student has 14 errors, the formula would look like this:

$$\dfrac{133 - 14}{133} = \dfrac{119}{133} = 89\%$$

- The self-correction rate is calculated by adding both errors and the number of self-corrections together and then dividing by the number of self-corrections, e.g., errors 6, self-corrections 3

$$\dfrac{6 + 3}{3} = \dfrac{9}{3} = \text{a S.C. rate of } 1 : 3$$

- In the next two columns write **MSV** beside every error and self-correction. The letters are an abbreviation for the cues that students use:

    M for meaning
    S for the structure of the sentence
    V for sources of visual information.

- Analyze each error. Circle the cueing system(s) the student used while reading:

    M if the student was trying to use meaning   (M) S V
    S if the student was trying to use language structure   M (S) V
    V if the student was trying to use visual cues   M S (V)

- To analyze a student's self-correction behaviors, first circle in the **Errors** column the cueing systems that the student used when they made the incorrect response. Then circle the cues the student used to change the incorrect response to a correct one in the **Self-correction** column.
- Count the number of times each type of cue was used, and record the total at the bottom of the last two columns. This information will give insight into the dominant cues being used by the student.

> Analyzed information from the Reading Record is summarized and recommendations for teaching objectives are set. Objectives will relate to the student's reading behaviors, e.g.:

- Are concepts about print firmly established?
- Does the student search for meaning?
- Does the student confirm structure so that the reading makes sense?
- Does the student use letters and letter-sound relationships to confirm visual information?
- Is there evidence of self-monitoring?
- Is the student self-correcting?
- Is there evidence of fluency and phrasing in the student's oral reading?

Questions

By responding to the comprehension questions on the Assessment Record, students will demonstrate the depth of meaning that they have gained from reading the text. Besides recalling and exploring details from the text, students are invited to use their own background knowledge and experiences as they respond to the questions. If students do not respond with the given answer, note their response in the space provided. Use your best judgement to decide if the alternate answer is appropriate or not.

- The students are asked the prepared questions **after** they have completed the reading record and finished reading the story.
- There are 3 questions for levels 1–10, 4 questions for levels 11-20 and 5 questions for levels 21–30.
- The questions will include:

    Literal comprehension which requires students to recall or locate the information in the text.

    Inferential comprehension which challenges students to link meaning with other sources of information either in or beyond the text.

Some questions in levels 21–30 will challenge students to explain *generalizations or points of view*.

Rigby PM Benchmark Kit 2

Reading and Assessment Records

See pages 10-11 for guidelines on how to administer the assessment records.

Notes on running words

In the *Rigby PM Benchmark Kit* the number of running words in a Reading Record extract have been calculated following these rules:

- The words on the cover and title page are not counted.

- Compound words are counted as one word.

- Hyphenated words are counted as one word.

- Sounds such as *brmm brmm* are not counted as words.

- Numbers shown in numeral form, e.g., *1, 2, 3* are not counted as words; however, when they are spelled out, e.g., *one, two, three,* they are counted.

Level 5

Sample Reading Record

Name: Zack   **Age:** 5   **Date:** 12/6/02
Text: Little Teddy helps Mouse   **Level:** 5   **R. W:** 91
Accuracy: 94%   **S.C. Rate:** 1:2

Page	This story is about how Little Teddy helps Mouse.	E	S.C.	Errors MSV	Self corrections MSV
3	✓ and|SC ✓ ✓ ✓ ✓ Mouse said, "Little Teddy! Little Teddy! W- |A| |T ✓ ✓ ✓ Where are you going?"	1 1		Ⓜ Ⓢ V M S Ⓥ	Ⓜ Ⓢ Ⓥ
4	✓ ✓ ✓ ✓ ✓ start|SC ↓"I am going to the store," ✓ ✓ ✓ said Little Teddy.	1		Ⓜ Ⓢ Ⓥ	M S Ⓥ
	✓ ✓ ✓ ✓ ✓ ✓ "Can I come too?" said Mouse. ✓ ✓ ✓ ✓ ✓ ✓ ↓"Can I come to the store?" Voice pointing				
6	✓ ✓ said ✓ ✓ "Mouse! Mouse!" shouted Little Teddy. ✓ d- "Look down!|T	1 1		Ⓜ Ⓢ Ⓥ M S Ⓥ	
	✓ ✓ ✓ ✓ puddle|SC ✓ ↓Look down at the big |puddle."		1	Ⓜ Ⓢ V	Ⓜ Ⓢ Ⓥ
8	✓ ✓ ✓ ✓ R Mouse went into the puddle. No ✓ ✓ ✓ "Oh!|T Oh!" he said.	1		M S Ⓥ	
10	✓ ✓ ✓ ✓ ↓"Where am I?"said Mouse. ✓ ✓ ✓ puddle|SC ✓ ✓ ✓ ✓ "You are in the big |puddle," said Little Teddy.		1	Ⓜ Ⓢ V	Ⓜ Ⓢ Ⓥ
12	✓ ✓ ✓ ✓ ✓ Mouse said, "Look at me!" ✓ ✓ ✓ ✓ the|SC ✓ "Come on, Mouse," said Little| Teddy. ✓ ✓ ↓"Come here."	1		Ⓜ Ⓢ V	M S Ⓥ
14	✓ ✓ ✓ ✓ ✓ ✓ Little Teddy and Mouse went home.				
16	Th- |T ✓ ✓ ✓ ✓ ✓ "Thank you, Little Teddy," said Mouse.	1		M S Ⓥ	
	Total	5	5	⑥ ⑥ ⑥	③ ③ ⑤

Level 5: *Little Teddy helps Mouse*

Sample Assessment Record

Name: Zack

Analysis of retelling *(meaning, main ideas, coherence, vocabulary, reference to text)*

Meaning firmly established, e.g., Teddy went shopping. Mouse wanted to go, too. Main ideas retold in sequential order. Meaning sometimes linked to own experiences, i.e. Mouse didn't look where he was going. Sometimes I fall down, too. An appropriate conclusion provided, i.e. He washed Mouse to get the mud off.

Questions to check for understanding *(check if understanding acceptable)*

1. Where was Little Teddy going?

   Response: (to the store) ✓

2. Who fell in the puddle?

   Response: (Mouse) ✓

3. Why do you think Mouse went home with Little Teddy?

   Response: (to get cleaned up)   to wash the mud off ✓

Reading level

Accuracy level: $\dfrac{91-5}{91}$ = 94.5%

Self-correction rate: $\dfrac{5+5}{5}$ = $\dfrac{10}{5}$ = 1:2

Reading level *(with understanding):* Easy / (Instructional) / Hard

Analysis of reading behaviors *(print concepts, meaning cues, structural cues, visual information, self-monitoring, self-correcting, fluency, expression)*

Concepts about print are firmly established. Meaning cues are frequently used to predict text structure. Self-monitoring strategies involving cross-checking meaning with visual sources of information often lead to self-correction. Sometimes returns to beginning of the sentence to check and confirm. Repeats are usually read with voice pointing monotone.

Recommendations:
- Continue to focus upon self-monitoring strategies.
- Encourage reading of familiar texts with fluency and phrasing.
- Extend recognition of high-frequency words, e.g., where, shouted

Teacher: E.V. Nelley   **Date benchmark assessment completed:** 12/6/02

Level 1

Reading Record

Name: _____ Age: _____ Date: _____

Text: __On the table_____ Level: __1__ R. W: __56__

Accuracy: _____ S.C. Rate: _____

Page	This story is about a girl and her toys.	E	S.C.	Errors MSV	Self corrections MSV
2	The little car is on the table.				
4	The little doll is on the table.				
6	The little boat is on the table.				
8	The little truck is on the table.				
10	The little ball is on the table.				
12	The little plane is on the table.				
14	The little bus is on the table.				
16	The teddy bear is on the table.				
		Total			

Level 1: *On the table*

Assessment Record

Name: _____

Analysis of retelling *(meaning, main ideas, coherence, vocabulary, reference to text)*

_____

Questions to check for understanding *(check if understanding acceptable)*

1. Where did the girl put the toys?

   Response: (on the table) ☐

2. What was the last toy that she put on the table?

   Response: (the teddy bear) ☐

3. Which toy would you like to play with?

   Response: (answers will vary) ☐

_____

Reading level

Accuracy level: $\dfrac{56 - }{56}$ = _____ %

Self-correction rate: _____ = _____ = 1:

Reading level *(with understanding):* Easy / Instructional / Hard

_____

Analysis of reading behaviors *(print concepts, meaning cues, structural cues, visual information, self-monitoring, self-correcting, fluency, expression)*

Recommendations:

Teacher: _____   Date benchmark assessment completed: _____

Reading Record

Level 2

Name: _____ Age: _____ Date: _____

Text: **At the zoo** _____ Level: **2** R. W: **43**

Accuracy: _____ S.C. Rate: _____

Page	This story is about a boy and his mom and their day at the zoo.	E	S.C.	Errors MSV	Self corrections MSV
2	"Come here!" said Mom.				
4	"Come and see the elephant."				
6	"Come here!" said Mom.				
8	"Come and see the bears."				
10	"Come here!" said Mom.				
12	"Come and see the zebras."				
14	"Come and see the monkeys," said Mom. "Look at the monkeys."				
16	"Look at the **baby** monkey!"				
		Total			

Reading Record © Rigby, 2002.
This page may be photocopied for educational use within the purchasing institution.

Level 2: *At the zoo*

Assessment Record

Name: _____

Analysis of retelling *(meaning, main ideas, coherence, vocabulary, reference to text)*

_____

_____

Questions to check for understanding *(check if understanding acceptable)*

1. Where did the boy and his mother go to see the animals?

   Response: (to the zoo) ☐

2. What were some of the animals that they saw?

   Response: (elephant, bears, zebras, monkeys) ☐

3. Which animal do you think the boy liked best?

   Response: (the baby monkey) ☐

Reading level

Accuracy level: $\dfrac{43 - }{43}$ = _____ %

Self-correction rate: _____ = _____ = 1: ___

Reading level *(with understanding):*   Easy / Instructional / Hard

Analysis of reading behaviors *(print concepts, meaning cues, structural cues, visual information, self-monitoring, self-correcting, fluency, expression)*

Recommendations:

Teacher: _____   Date benchmark assessment completed: _____

Level 3

Reading Record

Name: _____ Age: _____ Date: _____

Text: _Kate goes to a farm_ Level: __3__ R. W: __69__

Accuracy: _____ S.C. Rate: _____

Page	This story is about Kate and her dad who go to a farm.	E	S.C.	Errors MSV	Self corrections MSV
3	Kate is at a farm. Dad is at the farm, too.				
5	Dad said, "Come here, Kate. Look at the horse."				
7	"No," said Kate. "The horse is too big!"				
9	"Come here, Kate," said Dad. "Here is a cow."				
11	"Come on, Kate," said Dad. "No," said Kate. "The cow is too big!"				
13	"Look, Dad," said Kate. "Here is a cat."				
15	"Come here, Dad," said Kate. "Look!"				
16	"Look at the **little** kittens!"				
	Total				

24

Level 3: *Kate goes to a farm*

Assessment Record

Name: _____

Analysis of retelling (meaning, main ideas, coherence, vocabulary, reference to text)

_____

Questions to check for understanding (check if understanding acceptable)

1. Who went to the farm?

    Response: (Kate and her dad) ☐

2. Why didn't Kate want to go near the horse?

    Response: (it was too big) ☐

3. Why do you think Kate was happy to go and see the kittens?

    Response: (they were little) ☐

Reading level

Accuracy level: $\dfrac{69 - }{69}$ = _____ %

Self-correction rate: _____ = _____ = 1: _____

Reading level *(with understanding):* Easy / Instructional / Hard

Analysis of reading behaviors (print concepts, meaning cues, structural cues, visual information, self-monitoring, self-correcting, fluency, expression)

Recommendations:

Teacher: _____   Date benchmark assessment completed: _____

Level 4

Reading Record

Name: _____ Age: _____ Date: _____

Text: __The big plane_____ Level: __4__ R. W: __83__

Accuracy: _____ S.C. Rate: _____

Page	This story is about Ben and his mom and their trip to the airport.	E	S.C.	Errors MSV	Self corrections MSV
2	Ben and Mom looked for the big plane.				
4	"Here comes the big plane," said Ben. "Dad is in the plane."				
6	"Look, Mom!" said Ben. "The big plane is here."				
8	Mom and Ben looked for Dad. "I can not see Dad," said Ben.				
10	Mom and Ben looked and looked for Dad. Ben said to Mom, "Can you see Dad?"				
12	"No!" said Mom. "I can not see Dad." "Dad is **not** in the plane," said Ben.				
14	"Look, Ben," said Mom.				
16	"Here comes Dad!" shouted Ben.				
		Total			

26

Reading Record © Rigby, 2002.
This page may be photocopied for educational use within the purchasing institution.

Rigby PM Benchmark

Level 4: *The big plane*

Assessment Record

Name:

Analysis of retelling *(meaning, main ideas, coherence, vocabulary, reference to text)*

Questions to check for understanding *(check if understanding acceptable)*

1. Who was looking for the big plane?

   Response: (Ben and his mom)

2. Who was coming in the big plane?

   Response: (Ben's dad)

3. Dad is carrying a big package. What do you think might be in it?

   Response: (answers will vary)

Reading level

Accuracy level: $\dfrac{83 - }{83}$ = ____ %

Self-correction rate: _____ = _____ = 1:

Reading level *(with understanding):* Easy / Instructional / Hard

Analysis of reading behaviors *(print concepts, meaning cues, structural cues, visual information, self-monitoring, self-correcting, fluency, expression)*

Recommendations:

Teacher: Date benchmark assessment completed:

Level 5

Reading Record

Name: _____ Age: _____ Date: _____

Text: _Little Teddy helps Mouse_____ Level: __5__ R. W: __91__

Accuracy: _____ S.C. Rate: _____

Page	This story is about how Little Teddy helps Mouse.	E	S.C.	Errors MSV	Self corrections MSV
3	Mouse said, "Little Teddy! Little Teddy! Where are you going?"				
5	"I am going to the store," said Little Teddy. "Can I come too?" said Mouse. "Can I come to the store?"				
7	"Mouse! Mouse!" shouted Little Teddy. "Look down! Look at the big puddle!"				
9	Mouse went into the puddle. "Oh! Oh!" he said.				
11	"Where am I?" said Mouse. "You are in the big puddle," said Little Teddy.				
13	Mouse said, "Look at me!" "Come on, Mouse," said Little Teddy. "Come here."				
15	Little Teddy and Mouse went home.				
16	"Thank you, Little Teddy," said Mouse.				
	Total				

Level 5: *Little Teddy helps Mouse*

Assessment Record

Name: _____

Analysis of retelling *(meaning, main ideas, coherence, vocabulary, reference to text)*

_____

Questions to check for understanding *(check if understanding acceptable)*

1. Where was Little Teddy going?
   Response: (to the store)   ☐

2. Who fell in the puddle?
   Response: (Mouse)   ☐

3. Why do you think Mouse went home with Little Teddy?
   Response: (to get cleaned up)   ☐

Reading level

Accuracy level: $\dfrac{91 - \_\_\_}{91}$ = _____ %

Self-correction rate: _____ = _____ = 1: _____

Reading level *(with understanding):*   Easy / Instructional / Hard

Analysis of reading behaviors *(print concepts, meaning cues, structural cues, visual information, self-monitoring, self-correcting, fluency, expression)*

Recommendations:

Teacher: _____   Date benchmark assessment completed: _____

Level 6

Reading Record

Name: _____ Age: _____ Date: _____

Text: __Nick's snowman_____ Level: __6__ R. W: __104__

Accuracy: _____ S.C. Rate: _____

Page	This story is about what happens when Nick and Sally try to build a snowman.	E	S.C.	Errors MSV	Self corrections MSV
2	"Sally!" shouted Nick. "Look at the snow!"				
4	Nick and Sally went downstairs. They went to see the snow.				
6	"Look at this big snowball," said Nick. "My little snowball can go up here," said Sally. "A snowman!" said Nick. "This is a snowman!"				
8	"Here are the sticks for the snowman," said Nick. "Oh, no! Here come the dogs." Sally said to the dogs, "Go away!"				
11	The dogs went up to Nick. They looked at the stick. "Go away," said Nick.				
13	"You are naughty dogs!" shouted Nick. "Go inside. This stick is for my snowman."				
15	Sally said, "Come here, dogs. The sticks are not for you."				
	Allow student to finish reading the book.	Total			

Rigby PM Benchmark

Level 6: *Nick's snowman*

Assessment Record

Name: _____

Analysis of retelling *(meaning, main ideas, coherence, vocabulary, reference to text)*

_____

_____

Questions to check for understanding *(check if understanding acceptable)*

1. Where did Sally put the little snowball? ☐

   Response: (on top of the big snowball)

2. What were the sticks for? ☐

   Response: (for the snowman's arms)

3. Why do you think the dogs wanted to get the sticks? ☐

   Response: (to play with or chew on)

Reading level

Accuracy level: $\dfrac{104 - }{104}$ = _____ %

Self-correction rate: _____ = _____ = 1: _____

Reading level *(with understanding):*   Easy / Instructional / Hard

Analysis of reading behaviors *(print concepts, meaning cues, structural cues, visual information, self-monitoring, self-correcting, fluency, expression)*

_____

_____

Recommendations: _____

Teacher: _____   Date benchmark assessment completed: _____

Level 7

Reading Record

Name:	Age:	Date:
Text: Baby Bear and the big fish	Level: 7	R.W: 100
	Accuracy:	S.C. Rate:

Page	This story is about the bear family, and their names are Father Bear, Mother Bear, and Baby Bear.	E	S.C.	Errors MSV	Self corrections MSV
3	The bears liked to go fishing down at the river. "I can see some fish today," said Baby Bear. "Here they come."				
5	Mother Bear went into the river, and she got some fish. Father Bear got some fish, too. "We are good at fishing," said Father Bear.				
7	"Where is a fish for **me**?" said Baby Bear.				
9	"I can see a big fish," said Father Bear. "This fish is for me!" shouted Baby Bear.				
11	Baby Bear got the big fish in the net. Away went the fish. Baby Bear and the fish went up the river!				
13	"Help! Help!" shouted Baby Bear.				
	Allow student to finish reading the book.	Total			

Level 7: *Baby Bear and the big fish*

Rigby PM Benchmark

Assessment Record

Name: _____

Analysis of retelling *(meaning, main ideas, coherence, vocabulary, reference to text)*

_____

_____

Questions to check for understanding *(check if understanding acceptable)*

1. Where did the bears go fishing? ☐

   Response: (in the river)

2. Who saved Baby Bear? ☐

   Response: (Father Bear)

3. Why do you think Baby Bear called out, "Help! Help!"? ☐

   Response: (the big fish was carrying him away and he was frightened)

Reading level

Accuracy level: $\dfrac{100 - }{100}$ = _____ %

Self-correction rate: _____ = _____ = 1:

Reading level *(with understanding):* Easy / Instructional / Hard

Analysis of reading behaviors *(print concepts, meaning cues, structural cues, visual information, self-monitoring, self-correcting, fluency, expression)*

Recommendations:

Teacher: _____   Date benchmark assessment completed: _____

Level 8

Reading Record

Name: _____ Age: _____ Date: _____

Text: __My big sister_____ Level: __8__ R. W: __110__

Text type: __Informative_____ Accuracy: _____ S.C. Rate: _____

Page	This book is about a girl who has an older sister.	E	S.C.	Errors MSV	Self corrections MSV
2	I like my sister. She is 9, and I am 6. She is big, and I am little.				
4	We like to play at home. My sister gets the red ball, and we play with it by the trees.				
6	I get the ball, and I run away with it. My sister runs after me, and she gets the ball back.				
8	On wet days, we stay inside. We read some books. My big sister is good at reading. She reads books to me.				
10	I can read some of the books, too. My big sister helps me.				
12	We go to the park with Mom and Dad. We run all the way to the big slide.				
	Allow student to finish reading the book.	Total			

Level 8: *My big sister*

Assessment Record

Name: _____

Analysis of retelling (meaning, main ideas, coherence, vocabulary, reference to text)

_____

Questions to check for understanding (check if understanding acceptable)

1. How old is the big sister in the story?

   Response: (nine) ☐

2. What did the girls play on at the park?

   Response: (on the slide) ☐

3. Why do you think the big sister takes care of her little sister?

   Response: (answers will vary) ☐

Reading level

Accuracy level: $\dfrac{110 - }{110}$ = _____ %

Self-correction rate: _____ = _____ = 1: _____

Reading level (with understanding): Easy / Instructional / Hard

Analysis of reading behaviors (print concepts, meaning cues, structural cues, visual information, self-monitoring, self-correcting, fluency, expression)

Recommendations:

Teacher: _____ Date benchmark assessment completed: _____

Level 9

Reading Record

Name: _____ Age: _____ Date: _____

Text: **Clever Little Dinosaur** Level: **9** R. W: **107**

Accuracy: _____ S.C. Rate: _____

Page	This story is about what happens when Little Dinosaur wakes up Big Dinosaur.	E	S.C.	Errors MSV	Self corrections MSV
3	Little Dinosaur came out of his hole. "I can't see Big Dinosaur today," he said. "I will go for a walk. I will go down to the river."				
5	Little Dinosaur liked eating dragonflies down by the river. A green dragonfly came out of the forest. Little Dinosaur ran after it. He jumped up at it again and again.				
6	Little Dinosaur jumped on Big Dinosaur's tail. Oh, no! This made Big Dinosaur wake up!				
8	Big Dinosaur got up. He ran after Little Dinosaur.				
9	**"Help!"** cried Little Dinosaur.				
11	Little Dinosaur had to get away. He ran into the forest. "Big Dinosaur can't run fast in the forest," he said.				
	Allow student to finish reading the book.	Total			

Level 9: *Clever Little Dinosaur*

Assessment Record

Name: _____

Analysis of retelling *(meaning, main ideas, coherence, vocabulary, reference to text)*

_____

Questions to check for understanding *(check if understanding acceptable)*

1. What did Little Dinosaur like to eat?

   Response: (dragonflies) ☐

2. Why couldn't Big Dinosaur run fast in the forest?

   Response: (the trees got in his way) ☐

3. Why do you think Little Dinosaur jumped on Big Dinosaur?

   Response: (he wasn't watching where he was going and jumped on his tail by accident) ☐

Reading level

Accuracy level: $\dfrac{107 - }{107}$ _____ %

Self-correction rate: _____ = _____ = 1:

Reading level *(with understanding):*   Easy / Instructional / Hard

Analysis of reading behaviors *(print concepts, meaning cues, structural cues, visual information, self-monitoring, self-correcting, fluency, expression)*

Recommendations:

Teacher: _____ Date benchmark assessment completed: _____

Level 10

Reading Record

Name: _____ Age: _____ Date: _____

Text: __The helpful bulldozer_____ Level: __10__ R. W: __116__

Accuracy: _____ S.C. Rate: _____

Page	This story is about a blue bus, a helicopter, and a bulldozer who are friends.	E	S.C.	Errors MSV	Self corrections MSV
2	The blue bus went up the road to town. The helicopter saw the bus. He came flying down.				
4	"A tree has come down on the road by the big hill," said the helicopter. "You can't go to town today!" "But I **have** to go to town," said the bus.				
6	"Come and have a look at the tree," said the helicopter. "I will show you where it is."				
7	They went to see the tree.				
8	"Oh, yes!" said the bus. "That tree **is** in my way. Who can help me?"				
9	"I will go and get the bulldozer," said the helicopter. "He is making a new road down by the river. He can help you." Away went the helicopter.				
	Allow student to finish reading the book.	Total			

Level 10: *The helpful bulldozer*

Assessment Record

Name: _____

Analysis of retelling *(meaning, main ideas, coherence, vocabulary, reference to text)*

_____

Questions to check for understanding *(check if understanding acceptable)*

1. Where was the blue bus going?

   Response: (to town) ☐

2. Why did the helicopter go and get the bulldozer?

   Response: (to move the tree that was blocking the road) ☐

3. Why do you think the helicopter saw the tree before the bus saw it?

   Response: (because he was flying up above the big hill) ☐

Reading level

Accuracy level: $\dfrac{116 - }{116}$ = _____ %

Self-correction rate: _____ = _____ = 1: _____

Reading level *(with understanding):* Easy / Instructional / Hard

Analysis of reading behaviors *(print concepts, meaning cues, structural cues, visual information, self-monitoring, self-correcting, fluency, expression)*

Recommendations:

Teacher: _____ **Date benchmark assessment completed:** _____

Level 11

Reading Record

Name: _____ Age: _____ Date: _____

Text: __Tom's train ride_____ Level: __11__ R. W: __120__

Accuracy: _____ S.C. Rate: _____

Page	This story is about a train ride, and the people in the story are Tom and his mom.	E	S.C.	Errors MSV	Self corrections MSV
3	One day, Tom and his mother went to a park. "Look, Mom," said Tom. "I can see some children having a ride on a little train." Tom and Mom went over to the fence.				
5	The children waved to Tom, and he waved back. "They are having a good ride," said Tom. "But I can't go on that train. I can't sit in it by myself."				
7	Tom said, "Look, Mom! I can see a wheelchair. One of the children at the park has a wheelchair, too!"				
9	Then Tom saw a yellow train. "A girl is sitting in a big seat at the back of the train," he said.				
11	The children got off the train. But the girl stayed in the seat.				
	Allow student to finish reading the book.	Total			

Level 11: *Tom's train ride*

Assessment Record

Name: _____

Analysis of retelling *(meaning, main ideas, coherence, vocabulary, reference to text)*

_____

_____

Questions to check for understanding *(check if understanding acceptable)*

1. Where did Tom and his mother go to see the little trains?

   Response: (to a park)   ☐

2. What did Tom do when the children waved to him?

   Response: (he waved back)   ☐

3. Where did Tom sit on the train?

   Response: (in a big seat at the back)   ☐

4. Why do you think Tom was able to have a ride on the yellow train?

   Response: (because it had a special seat)   ☐

Reading level

Accuracy level: $\dfrac{120 - \_\_\_\_}{120}$ = _____ %

Self-correction rate: _____ = _____ = 1: _____

Reading level *(with understanding):*   Easy / Instructional / Hard

Analysis of reading behaviors *(print concepts, meaning cues, structural cues, visual information, self-monitoring, self-correcting, fluency, expression)*

_____

_____

Recommendations: _____

Teacher: _____   Date benchmark assessment completed: _____

Level 12

Reading Record

Name: _____ Age: _____ Date: _____

Text: _Buying a new house_ Level: __12__ R. W: __121__

Text type: _Journal_ Accuracy: _____ S.C. Rate: _____

Page	This book is about a family who wants to buy a new house. It is told by a boy who is writing in his journal.	E	S.C.	Errors MSV	Self corrections MSV
2	Mom said that Grandma was coming to stay with us. She will be staying with us for a long time. I love my Grandma.				
4	Mom and Dad want to buy a bigger house for us. Our house has two bedrooms. I sleep in this bedroom with my brother, Ben. We are going to buy a new house with a bedroom for Grandma.				
6	Today we went for a ride in the car. We saw lots of houses. I liked the white house best.				
8	We went to see the white house again. We looked over the fence. We saw a lot of grass for Ben and me to play on. We will go inside the house in the morning.				
10	We went inside the house today.				
	Allow student to finish reading the book.	Total			

Rigby PM Benchmark

Level 12: *Buying a new house*

Assessment Record

Name:

Analysis of retelling *(meaning, main ideas, coherence, vocabulary, reference to text)*

_____

Questions to check for understanding *(check if understanding acceptable)*

1. Who was coming to stay with the family?

    Response: (Grandma) ☐

2. Why did Dad and Mom want to buy a bigger house?

    Response: (to have a bedroom for Grandma) ☐

3. Which house did they buy?

    Response: (the white house) ☐

4. Why do you think Grandma was coming to stay for a long time?

    Response: (answers will vary) ☐

Reading level

Accuracy level: $\dfrac{121 - }{121}$ = _____ %

Self-correction rate: _____ = _____ = 1:

Reading level *(with understanding):*   Easy / Instructional / Hard

Analysis of reading behaviors *(print concepts, meaning cues, structural cues, visual information, self-monitoring, self-correcting, fluency, expression)*

Recommendations:

Teacher: Date benchmark assessment completed:

Assessment Record © Rigby, 2002.
This page may be photocopied for educational use within the purchasing institution.

Level 13

Reading Record

Name: _____ Age: _____ Date: _____

Text: The best runner Level: 13 R. W: 133

Accuracy: _____ S.C. Rate: _____

Page	This story is about some children named Rachel, Anna, and James who are running a race at school.	E	S.C.	Errors MSV	Self corrections MSV
3	One morning, Mrs. Green and her class went to the park. "Who likes running?" she said. "We do!" the children shouted.				
5	"Can we run to the swings and back again?" said Rachel. "Yes," said Mrs. Green. "You can start at this line." Rachel said to Anna, "I want to be **first**, today."				
7	Mrs. Green called out to the children, "Are you ready? **GO!**" Rachel and Anna ran fast. James was a good runner, too. "Look out, Rachel!" called Anna. "James is coming!"				
9	Rachel and Anna ran very fast, but James ran faster still. **He** was first. "James, you are the best runner," said Rachel. But she was not very happy. She had wanted to be first today.				
11	Rachel looked at Mrs. Green. "Can we go for a **longer** run this time?" said Rachel.				
	Allow student to finish reading the book.	Total			

44

Reading Record © Rigby, 2002.
This page may be photocopied for educational use within the purchasing institution.

Level 13: *The best runner*

Assessment Record

Name:

Analysis of retelling *(meaning, main ideas, coherence, vocabulary, reference to text)*

Questions to check for understanding *(check if understanding acceptable)*

1. Where did Mrs. Green take her class?
   Response: (to the park)

2. Who was the best runner when the children ran to the swings and back?
   Response: (James)

3. What happened to a boy just as they started to run around the park?
   Response: (he fell down)

4. Why do you think Rachel wanted to run a much longer race?
   Response: (answers will vary)

Reading level

Accuracy level: $\dfrac{133 - }{133}$ = _____ %

Self-correction rate: _____ = _____ = 1: _____

Reading level *(with understanding)*: Easy / Instructional / Hard

---

Analysis of reading behaviors *(print concepts, meaning cues, structural cues, visual information, self-monitoring, self-correcting, fluency, expression)*

Recommendations:

Teacher: _____ Date benchmark assessment completed: _____

Level 14

Reading Record

Name: _____ Age: _____ Date: _____

Text: Little Hen, Mouse, and Rabbit Level: 14 R. W: 140

Accuracy: _____ S.C. Rate: _____

Page	This story is about three friends, Little Hen, Mouse, and Rabbit, who meet a hungry fox.	E	S.C.	Errors MSV	Self corrections MSV
2	Little Hen, Mouse, and Rabbit lived in a house by the woods. Little Hen did all the work in the house.				
3	Mouse and Rabbit sat on their chairs all day long. They were lazy!				
4	One morning, Little Hen went upstairs to make the beds. Mouse and Rabbit were asleep on their chairs. The door was open, and a hungry fox came in.				
5	Fox pushed Mouse and Rabbit into his bag, and tied it up.				
6	Fox ran off into the woods. His bag was heavy. He put it down on the ground. Then he went to sleep under a tree.				
8	Little Hen came downstairs. Mouse was not there! Rabbit was gone too! She ran into the woods to look for them.				
9	Little Hen saw Fox, and she saw the bag. A tail was coming out of a hole in the bag.				
	Allow student to finish reading the book.	Total			

Level 14: *Little Hen, Mouse, and Rabbit*

Assessment Record

Name:

Analysis of retelling *(meaning, main ideas, coherence, vocabulary, reference to text)*

Questions to check for understanding *(check if understanding acceptable)*

1. At the beginning of the story, who did all the work in the house?

   Response: (Little Hen)

2. What did Fox do to Mouse and Rabbit?

   Response: (pushed them in a bag)

3. Why did Fox put the bag down on the ground?

   Response: (the bag was heavy and he was tired)

4. Little Hen saw a tail coming out of the bag. Whom do you think it belonged to?

   Response: (Mouse)

Reading level

Accuracy level: $\dfrac{140-}{140}$ = ____ %

Self-correction rate: _____ = _____ = 1:

Reading level *(with understanding):* Easy / Instructional / Hard

Analysis of reading behaviors *(print concepts, meaning cues, structural cues, visual information, self-monitoring, self-correcting, fluency, expression)*

Recommendations:

Teacher: Date benchmark assessment completed:

Level 15

Reading Record

Name: _____ Age: _____ Date: _____

Text: __Skip Goes to the Rescue_____ Level: __15__ R. W: __135__

Accuracy: _____ S.C. Rate: _____

Page	This story is about a sea plane named Skip and the pilot named Jess.	E	S.C.	Errors MSV	Self corrections MSV
2	Jess climbed into her sea plane. "I have just had a phone call," she told the little plane. "We have work to do, Skip. We will have to hurry."				
4	Jess started Skip's engine. "We are going over to the island," she said. "A boy has broken his arm. He needs our help." Skip went faster and faster over the water. Then the little sea plane went up into the air.				
6	Soon the little plane came to the island. Jess looked down. "I can't see the boy," she shouted. "Fly around the island, Skip."				
7	Skip flew slowly around the island. Then Jess saw some people on the beach. They were waving. A boy was sitting on the ground.				
8	"Look, Skip!" shouted Jess. "There is the boy! But he is down on the beach by the rocks.				
	Allow student to finish reading the book. Total				

48

Level 15: *Skip Goes to the Rescue*

Assessment Record

Name: _____

Analysis of retelling *(meaning, main ideas, coherence, vocabulary, reference to text)*

_____

_____

Questions to check for understanding *(check if understanding acceptable)*

1. What was the name of the sea plane? ☐

    Response: (Skip)

2. Why did Jess and Skip have to go over to the island? ☐

    Response: (a boy had broken his arm and needed help)

3. Why did Skip land at the far end of the beach? ☐

    Response: (to avoid the rocks)

4. How do you think the boy might have broken his arm? ☐

    Response: (answers will vary)

Reading level

Accuracy level: $\dfrac{135-\rule{1cm}{0.15mm}}{135} = \rule{1cm}{0.15mm}$ %

Self-correction rate: _____ = _____ = 1:

Reading level *(with understanding)*:   Easy / Instructional / Hard

Analysis of reading behaviors *(print concepts, meaning cues, structural cues, visual information, self-monitoring, self-correcting, fluency, expression)*

_____

_____

Recommendations:

_____

Teacher: _____   Date benchmark assessment completed: _____

Level 16

Reading Record

Name: _____ Age: _____ Date: _____

Text: __The Classroom Play_____ Level: __16__ R. W: __132__

Accuracy: _____ S.C. Rate: _____

Page	This story is about a school play, and the names of the characters in it are Emma, Matthew, and Miss Hill.	E	S.C.	Errors MSV	Self corrections MSV
2	Miss Hill looked at the children in her class.				
3	She said to Emma, "You can be Little Red Riding Hood in our play." Emma smiled at her brother, Matthew, who was sitting beside her. "I hope I can be the Big Bad Wolf," said Matthew.				
4	But Miss Hill picked Sam to be the wolf.				
5	Matthew was not happy. Miss Hill said, "You can take your books home, and practice the play. The children from Room 10 will be coming to see it in the morning."				
6	After school, Emma took her book out of her bag. Then she said, "Can you help me practice the play, Matthew?" But Matthew was still not feeling very happy. "I wanted to be the wolf," he said.				
9	"Oh, **please**, Matthew," said Emma. "I need you to help me!"				
	Allow student to finish reading the book.	Total			

Level 16: *The Classroom Play*

Assessment Record

Name: _____

Analysis of retelling *(meaning, main ideas, coherence, vocabulary, reference to text)*

_____

Questions to check for understanding *(check if understanding acceptable)*

1. Who was Emma going to be in the play? ☐

   Response: (Little Red Riding Hood)

2. Who did Matthew want to be in the play? ☐

   Response: (the Big Bad Wolf)

3. Why did Miss Hill say that the children could take their books home? ☐

   Response: (to practice the play)

4. Why do you think the children cheered when Matthew chased Emma around the classroom? ☐

   Response: (answers will vary)

Reading level

Accuracy level: $\dfrac{132-}{132}$ = _____ %

Self-correction rate: _____ = _____ = 1:

Reading level *(with understanding):*   Easy / Instructional / Hard

Analysis of reading behaviors *(print concepts, meaning cues, structural cues, visual information, self-monitoring, self-correcting, fluency, expression)*

Recommendations:

Teacher: _____   Date benchmark assessment completed: _____

Level 17

Reading Record

Name: _____ Age: _____ Date: _____

Text: __The Greedy Dog and the Bone_____ Level: __17__ R. W: __133__

Accuracy: _____ S.C. Rate: _____

Page	This story is about what happens when a little dog named Jip is given a big meaty bone.	E	S.C.	Errors MSV	Self corrections MSV
2	Once upon a time, there was a little dog named Jip. He was a greedy little dog.				
3	Every day, Jip would run across a field, over a bridge, and through some trees, until he came to a shop.				
4	One morning, a man at the shop gave Jip a bone. It was a big meaty bone. "This is the biggest bone I have ever seen," said Jip to himself. "I will take it home and hide it. No one else can have this bone. It is just for me." So off he went, back through the trees.				
6	Just as Jip was running through the trees, he heard a noise. "Oh no!" he said. "Someone is coming! This bone belongs to me. No one else can have it. I will have to run even faster."				
	Allow student to finish reading the book.	Total			

52

Reading Record © Rigby, 2002.
This page may be photocopied for educational use within the purchasing institution.

Level 17: *The Greedy Dog and the Bone*

Assessment Record

Name:

Analysis of retelling *(meaning, main ideas, coherence, vocabulary, reference to text)*

Questions to check for understanding *(check if understanding acceptable)*

1. What was Jip going to do with the bone when he got home?

   Response: (hide it and chew on it)

2. What did Jip say that tells us that he was a greedy dog?

   Response: (No one else can have this bone. It is just for me.)

3. Jip thought he saw another dog in the water. But what was he really looking at?

   Response: (his reflection)

4. Why do you think Jip said that he would never be greedy again?

   Response: (answers will vary)

Reading level

Accuracy level: $\frac{133-}{133}$ = ___ %

Self-correction rate: _____ = _____ = 1:

Reading level *(with understanding):* Easy / Instructional / Hard

Analysis of reading behaviors *(print concepts, meaning cues, structural cues, visual information, self-monitoring, self-correcting, fluency, expression)*

Recommendations:

Teacher: Date benchmark assessment completed:

Level 18

Reading Record

Name: _____ Age: _____ Date: _____

Text: __Harvest Mice_____ Level: __18__ R. W: __138__

Text type: __Informative_____ Accuracy: _____ S.C. Rate: _____

Suggestion:
a) The teacher reads the chapter headings to the student.
b) The student reads pages 2–5 aloud, before reading the assessment section.

Page	This nonfiction text is about harvest mice and how they live in wheat fields.	E	S.C.	Errors MSV	Self corrections MSV
6	Harvest mice eat all kinds of seeds. They like to eat wheat seeds. They hold the seeds in their front paws.				
7	Harvest mice like to eat berries, too. They eat insects. They eat new green leaves. Harvest mice eat **many** things.				
8	Harvest mice are always in danger, because many animals try to catch them. Foxes hunt them in the grass. Owls hunt them from the sky.				
9	But in the summer, harvest mice have a good place to hide. Foxes and owls cannot see them, or hear them, in tall, thick wheat.				
10	Harvest mice build their nests high up in the wheat, where they are safe. The mother mouse bends some long leaves. She pulls them around the wheat stalks with her teeth and paws. She works quickly, and soon the nest looks like a little ball of grass.				
	Allow student to finish reading the book.	Total			

Level 18: *Harvest Mice*

Assessment Record

Name: _____

Analysis of retelling *(meaning, main ideas, coherence, vocabulary, reference to text)*

_____

_____

Questions to check for understanding *(check if understanding acceptable)*

1. What do harvest mice use their tails for?

   Response: (to hold on to the wheat) ☐

2. What are some of the things that harvest mice eat?

   Response: (seeds, berries, insects, new green leaves, many things) ☐

3. Why are harvest mice always in danger?

   Response: (because many animals try to catch and eat them) ☐

4. Why do you think the nests of harvest mice are hard to see in a wheatfield?

   Response: (because the wheat is thick and the nests are made of wheat) ☐

Reading level

Accuracy level: $\dfrac{138-}{138}$ = _____ %

Self-correction rate: _____ = _____ = 1: ___

Reading level *(with understanding):* Easy / Instructional / Hard

Analysis of reading behaviors *(print concepts, meaning cues, structural cues, visual information, self-monitoring, self-correcting, fluency, expression)*

_____

_____

Recommendations:

Teacher: _____   Date benchmark assessment completed: _____

Level 19

Reading Record

Name: _____ Age: _____ Date: _____

Text: _The Old Cabin in the Forest_ Level: **19** R. W: **142**

Accuracy: _____ S.C. Rate: _____

Page	This story is about a bike ride to an old cabin in the forest, and the characters are Zack, his mom and dad, and his friend Mitch.	E	S.C.	Errors MSV	Self corrections MSV
2	Zack and his friend Mitch were going riding with Zack's parents. "We have decided to ride up to the old cabin, in the forest by the river," Zack said to Mitch. "It's a great place!" "Does anyone live there?" asked Mitch. "Not now," laughed Zack. "But I think wild cats hide under it sometimes."				
4	Soon they were ready. They set off along the river path. "Zack!" shouted Dad. "Don't ride too fast. Don't get too far ahead of us." "Keep on the path until you get to the forest," called Mom. "Wait for us there."				
6	At last, Zack and Mitch reached the place where the river path ended. Two different paths led into the forest. Zack's parents caught up with the boys. "Which way do we go?" asked Zack. "Follow the path on the left," said Mom. "Go past the picnic ground."				
	Allow student to finish reading the book.	Total			

Level 19:   *The Old Cabin in the Forest*

Assessment Record

Name:

Analysis of retelling *(meaning, main ideas, coherence, vocabulary, reference to text)*

Questions to check for understanding *(check if understanding acceptable)*

1. What did Zack think might be hiding under the old cabin?

   Response: (a wild cat)

2. Where did they ride before they got to the forest path?

   Response: (on the river path)

3. Which forest path did Mom tell the boys to follow?

   Response: (the path on the left)

4. Explain why it is important to stay on the path while in the forest.

   Response: (answers will vary)

Reading level

Accuracy level: $\dfrac{142-\_\_\_\_}{142} = \_\_\_\_ \%$

Self-correction rate: _____ = _____ = 1:

Reading level *(with understanding):*   **Easy / Instructional / Hard**

Analysis of reading behaviors *(print concepts, meaning cues, structural cues, visual information, self-monitoring, self-correcting, fluency, expression)*

Recommendations:

Teacher: Date benchmark assessment completed:

Assessment Record © Rigby, 2002.
This page may be photocopied for educational use within the purchasing institution.

Reading Record

Level 20

Name: _____ Age: _____ Date: _____

Text: _Leo the Lion Cub_____ Level: __20__ R. W: __153__

Accuracy: _____ S.C. Rate: _____

Page	This story is about a lion cub named Leo and what happens to him after his mother dies.	E	S.C.	Errors MSV	Self corrections MSV
2	Leo belonged to a large family of lions, called a pride. When he was only six weeks old, his mother died, so his aunts took care of him.				
3	Leo was the youngest and smallest cub in the pride. All of his cousins were bigger than he was. They often knocked him over when they played with him. They liked pouncing on his tail, and biting it. Leo had to be brave. He had to learn how to fight.				
4	Soon it was time for the pride to move on. The lions needed to find a new hunting ground.				
5	They padded off through the dry grass, one after the other. But Leo could not keep up. His little legs were too short.				
6	When Leo whimpered, one of his aunts stopped. He tried to catch up with her, but he could not walk fast enough. So she moved on without him.				
7	He was soon left behind.				
	Allow student to finish reading the book.	Total			

Rigby PM Benchmark

Level 20: *Leo the Lion Cub*

Assessment Record

Name:

Analysis of retelling *(meaning, main ideas, coherence, vocabulary, reference to text)*

Questions to check for understanding *(check if understanding acceptable)*

1. Who took care of Leo and fed him when his mother died?

   Response: (his aunts)

2. Leo belonged to a *pride of lions*. What does this mean?

   Response: (a large family of lions)

3. Why couldn't Leo keep up with the other lions in his family?

   Response: (His little legs were too short.)

4. Why do you think the lions had to move on to a new hunting ground?

   Response: (answers will vary)

Reading level

Accuracy level: $\frac{153-}{153} = \%$

Self-correction rate: _____ = _____ = 1:

Reading level *(with understanding):* Easy / Instructional / Hard

Analysis of reading behaviors *(print concepts, meaning cues, structural cues, visual information, self-monitoring, self-correcting, fluency, expression)*

Recommendations:

Teacher: Date benchmark assessment completed:

Reading Record

Name: _____ Age: _____ Date: _____
Text: __Kwan the Artist_____ Level: __21__ R. W: __204__
                                    Accuracy: _____ S.C. Rate: _____

This story is about Kwan who recently moved to this country and is new at school.	E	S.C.	Errors MSV MSV	Self corrections
Kwan sat in his classroom, feeling unhappy. He had been in this new country for only a few days, and so many things were different. His teacher was kind. She tried to explain things to him. But Kwan couldn't understand all the words that she was saying, and so he couldn't do his work very well. He wished that he could be good at something at this school. Kwan saw that some of the children were getting out paints and brushes. His teacher gave him a large piece of paper. Kwan loved painting! At last he knew what he was supposed to be doing! He smiled at his teacher, and she smiled back at him. Kwan decided to paint a picture of the plane that had brought him to his new country. He could remember just how it had looked. He took a brush and began to paint. As he worked, some of the children came to watch. Kwan was proud of his plane. It looked just like the real one. More children crowded around him. They all wanted to see his painting. Kwan couldn't understand everything they said, but he felt happy. He knew that they thought he was a very good artist.				
Total				

Level 21: *Kwan the Artist*

Assessment Record

Name: _____

Analysis of retelling *(meaning, main ideas, coherence, vocabulary, reference to text)*

_____

_____

Questions to check for understanding *(check if understanding acceptable)*

1. Why was Kwan feeling unhappy at the beginning of the story? ☐
   Response: (he was new and couldn't understand the teacher that well)

2. How long had Kwan been in this new country? ☐
   Response: (only a few days)

3. Why did Kwan smile when he saw the paints and brushes? ☐
   Response: (he loved painting and knew what to do)

4. Why do you think the children came to watch while Kwan painted? ☐
   Response: (because his painting was so good)

5. Explain why Kwan couldn't understand all the words that his teacher said. ☐
   Response: (he spoke another language and didn't know English that well)

Reading level

Accuracy level: $\dfrac{204-}{204}$ = _____ %

Self-correction rate: _____ = _____ = 1:

Reading level *(with understanding):* Easy / Instructional / Hard

Analysis of reading behaviors *(print concepts, meaning cues, structural cues, visual information, self-monitoring, self-correcting, fluency, expression)*

_____

Recommendations: _____

Teacher: _____ Date benchmark assessment completed: _____

Level 22

Reading Record

Name: _____ Age: _____ Date: _____
Text: **Trees on Our Planet** Level: **22** R. W: **207**
Text type: *Explanatory* Accuracy: _____ S.C. Rate: _____

This nonfiction text is about the importance of trees on our planet.	E	S.C.	Errors MSV	Self corrections MSV
People have been cutting down trees for thousands of years. The wood from trees is very useful. It can be used to build houses. It can be used to make tables and chairs and other furniture. Wood can be made into paper, too. But, all around the world, too many trees have been cut down. More and more houses have been built. Large cities have been built. In the past, people decided to turn huge areas of forest into farm land. They cut down millions of trees. They cleared the land quickly. But then some heavy rains came, and good soil on top of the ground was washed away. Nothing much would grow there. Today, people realize how important trees are. Their wide branches help to stop the rain from washing the topsoil away. Their strong roots hold the soil in place, even on steep mountains. And forests provide a home for many different kinds of animals. So people are now growing trees to replace the ones that have been cut down. When the young trees are strong enough, they are planted where they are needed most. But they take a long time to grow tall. We must all help to put trees back on our planet.				
Total				

Rigby PM Benchmark

Level 22: *Trees on Our Planet*

Assessment Record

Name: _____

Analysis of retelling (meaning, main ideas, coherence, vocabulary, reference to text)

_____

_____

Questions to check for understanding (check if understanding acceptable)

1. What are some useful things that can be made from wood? ☐
   Response: (houses, furniture, paper)

2. Why did people cut down millions of trees? ☐
   Response: (to clear the land for farming)

3. When heavy rains came, what happened to the land that had been cleared of trees? ☐
   Response: (the good topsoil was washed away)

4. How do trees protect the land? ☐
   Response: (Their roots hold the soil in place, and their branches help to stop rain from washing soil away.)

5. Explain why trees are so important for our planet. ☐
   Response: (answers will vary)

Reading level

Accuracy level: $\dfrac{207-\_\_\_\_}{207}$ = _____ %

Self-correction rate: _____ = _____ = 1: ____

Reading level (with understanding): Easy / Instructional / Hard

Analysis of reading behaviors (print concepts, meaning cues, structural cues, visual information, self-monitoring, self-correcting, fluency, expression)

Recommendations:

Teacher: _____ Date benchmark assessment completed: _____

Level 23

Reading Record

Name: _____ Age: _____ Date: _____

Text: __The Miller, His Son, and Their Donkey__ Level: __23__ R. W: __209__

Accuracy: _____ S.C. Rate: _____

This story is about a miller, his son, and their donkey who are going to a fair and the people they meet along the way.	E	S.C.	Errors MSV MSV	Self corrections
A miller and his son were taking their donkey to town to sell at a fair. After a while, they passed some women. One of the women said aloud, "Fancy walking, when you could be **riding** your donkey!" The miller told his son to ride the donkey. As they continued along the road, they came upon two men, deep in conversation. One of the men looked up and spoke loudly to the other. "That lazy boy has no respect for his father. The old man should be riding the donkey." When the miller heard this, he made his son dismount. Then he climbed onto the donkey instead. They hadn't gone far when they met another group of people. "You selfish old man!" cried a woman, pointing to the tired boy. At once, the miller pulled his son up beside him. The donkey trudged along with its heavy load. Soon they met a traveler. "Your donkey is exhausted," he frowned. "You'll have to carry it." The miller was so anxious to please the traveler that he tied the donkey's legs together. The miller and his son carried it on a pole between them. As they reached the edge of the town, people gathered around, laughing loudly at this odd sight.				
Allow student to finish reading the text.	Total			

Level 23: *The Miller, His Son, and Their Donkey*

Assessment Record

Name: _____

Analysis of retelling *(meaning, main ideas, coherence, vocabulary, reference to text)*

_____

_____

Questions to check for understanding *(check if understanding acceptable)*

1. Why was the miller taking his donkey to town?
   Response: (to sell at the fair) ☐

2. Why did one of the men say that the boy was lazy?
   Response: (he was riding the donkey while the father walked) ☐

3. When did the donkey become exhausted?
   Response: (when it was carrying both the miller and his son) ☐

4. What do you think was the silliest thing that the miller did?
   Response: (answers will vary) ☐

5. The miller tried to please everyone he met.
   Explain why this didn't work.
   Response: (because everyone had different ideas and opinions) ☐

Reading level

Accuracy level: $\frac{209-\_\_\_}{209}$ = _____ %

Self-correction rate: _____ = _____ = 1:____

Reading level *(with understanding):* **Easy / Instructional / Hard**

Analysis of reading behaviors *(print concepts, meaning cues, structural cues, visual information, self-monitoring, self-correcting, fluency, expression)*

_____

_____

Recommendations: _____

Teacher: _____ Date benchmark assessment completed: _____

Level 24

Reading Record

Name: _____ Age: _____ Date: _____

Text: __A New Skatepark__ Level: __24__ R. W: __209__

Text type: _____ Accuracy: _____ S.C. Rate: _____

This letter is written to the City Council asking the council to build a skatepark.	E	S.C.	Errors MSV	Self corrections MSV
Skateboarding is a very popular sport. Many children in Bay City enjoy it. But there are no parks in the city where we can skate safely. Last weekend, some children from our school were skating outside the stores on High Street. The store owners said that people couldn't get into the stores. They were very annoyed. Skateboarders have even damaged benches and the curb at the edge of the sidewalk. Some older people won't go to these stores any more. They are scared of being knocked down. Our class would like the council to build a skatepark. It could be built beside the new tennis courts. This would be a good place because there are enough lights for skating at night. The council should let children help with the design. A skatepark needs to be for children who are just learning. But it also needs to be for experienced skaters who can do more difficult moves. We think the park should have an oval track with ramps, steps, pipes, and low rails. It could have some barriers and a big pyramid in the center. Children could skate safely in a skatepark. Store owners and other people would be pleased too, because the area outside the stores wouldn't be dangerous.				
	Total			

Rigby PM Benchmark

Level 24: *A New Skatepark*

Assessment Record

Name: _____

Analysis of retelling *(meaning, main ideas, coherence, vocabulary, reference to text)*

_____

Questions to check for understanding *(check if understanding acceptable)*

1. What had the skateboarders damaged? ☐
   Response: (benches and the curb)

2. Why were some older people staying away from the High Street stores? ☐
   Response: (they were scared of being knocked down)

3. Why did the children think that it was a good idea to put the skatepark near the tennis courts? ☐
   Response: (the tennis courts had lights)

4. Ramps, steps, and pipes are features of a skatepark. What do you think are the most important features? Why? ☐
   Response: (answers will vary, but should include safety concerns)

5. Explain why the children wrote the email to the city council. ☐
   Response: (to persuade the city council to build a skatepark)

Reading level

Accuracy level: $\frac{209-\_\_\_\_}{209}$ = ____ %

Self-correction rate: _____ = _____ = 1: ___

Reading level *(with understanding):* Easy / Instructional / Hard

Analysis of reading behaviors *(print concepts, meaning cues, structural cues, visual information, self-monitoring, self-correcting, fluency, expression)*

Recommendations:

Teacher: _____ Date benchmark assessment completed: _____

Level 25

Reading Record

Name: _____ Age: _____ Date: _____

Text: **Beavers** _____ Level: **25** R. W: **200**

Text type: _Informative_ _____ Accuracy: _____ S.C. Rate: _____

This nonfiction text is about beavers and how they live.	E	S.C.	Errors MSV	Self corrections MSV
Beavers are excellent swimmers. They have webbed hind feet, waterproof fur, and flat hairless tails. They can close their nostrils and stay under water for up to 15 minutes. Adult beavers can be over a yard long. They have enormous front teeth for gnawing tree trunks. Beavers' teeth are strong and sharp, and keep growing throughout their lives. A beaver can chew through trunks that are half a yard across. Beavers build dams with the trees that they fell. When beavers start to make a new dam, they drag logs and branches into a stream, and bury the ends in stones and gravel. Then they pack more stones and mud around the logs to hold them firmly in place. Gaps are filled with smaller branches, waterweeds, and mud. The stream spreads out behind the dam to make a lake. Then the beaver and its mate cut down more trees, and build an island in the lake. The island is made of branches and mud. It is called a lodge. Inside the lodge, above water level, is a dry chamber where the beavers live and take care of their young. The only way out is through a tunnel with an underwater exit.				
Allow student to finish reading the text. **Total**				

Level 25: *Beavers*

Assessment Record

Name: _____

Analysis of retelling *(meaning, main ideas, coherence, vocabulary, reference to text)*

_____

Questions to check for understanding *(check if understanding acceptable)*

1. How do beavers cut down trees? ☐
   Response: (they chew through the trunks)

2. What do beavers do with the trees that they cut down? ☐
   Response: (they build dams)

3. When beavers build a dam across a stream, what happens to the water that cannot flow through? ☐
   Response: (it spreads out behind the dam to make a lake)

4. Why do you think beavers need to build themselves an island lodge? ☐
   Response: (answers should include shelter and safety)

5. What do people mean when they use the phrase *as busy as a beaver*? ☐
   Response: (beavers seem to work very hard and stay busy all the time)

Reading level

Accuracy level: $\dfrac{200-}{200}$ = _____ %

Self-correction rate: _____ = _____ = 1: _____

Reading level *(with understanding):* **Easy / Instructional / Hard**

Analysis of reading behaviors *(print concepts, meaning cues, structural cues, visual information, self-monitoring, self-correcting, fluency, expression)*

Recommendations:

Teacher: _____ Date benchmark assessment completed: _____

Level 26

Reading Record

Name: _____ Age: _____ Date: _____

Text: __A Great Sense of Smell_____ Level: __26__ R. W: __209__

Accuracy: _____ S.C. Rate: _____

This story is about a blind girl named Sophie who is staying the night at her friend Ella's house.	E	S.C.	Errors MSV	Self corrections MSV
Sophie felt for the handrail and then made her way carefully down the steps that led to the backyard. "Something smells delicious," she exclaimed. "Dad's cooking chicken on the grill," replied Ella. Sophie was blind. She often stayed with her friend Ella on weekends. The girls enjoyed each other's company, and did many things together. Later that evening, the girls were in their beds talking about the fishing trip that had been organized for the following day. After a while the girls drifted off to sleep. Several hours later Sophie stirred. She rolled over, but her instincts told her that something was wrong and she listened for noises. There were none, but she still had a very uneasy feeling. All of a sudden, Sophie realized what it was — she could smell smoke! She knew she must rouse Ella immediately. "Wake up, Ella!" she yelled. "I think the house is on fire!" Fortunately, Ella's parents heard Sophie's urgent cries, and they rushed into the bedroom. They all left the house, as quickly as possible, and Ella's dad ran next door to call the fire department. "Now the smoke alarm is going is going off!" said Ella, as they waited outside. "Wow, Sophie, you smelled the smoke even before the alarm detected it."				
Total				

Level 26: *A Great Sense of Smell*

Assessment Record

Name: _____

Analysis of retelling (meaning, main ideas, coherence, vocabulary, reference to text)

_____

Questions to check for understanding (check if understanding acceptable)

1. How is Sophie handicapped?
   Response: (she is blind) ☐

2. When did Sophie come to stay with her friend Ella?
   Response: (on weekends) ☐

3. What gave Sophie an uneasy feeling during the night?
   Response: (the smell of smoke) ☐

4. Why do you think Sophie's sense of smell was better than Ella's?
   Response: (since she couldn't see, Sophie probably relied on her sense of smell more than Ella did) ☐

5. When Sophie smelled smoke she knew she had to rouse Ella immediately. Explain why this was very important.
   Response: (answers will vary) ☐

Reading level

Accuracy level: $\dfrac{209-}{209}$ = _____ %

Self-correction rate: _____ = _____ = 1:

Reading level *(with understanding):* Easy / Instructional / Hard

Analysis of reading behaviors (print concepts, meaning cues, structural cues, visual information, self-monitoring, self-correcting, fluency, expression)

Recommendations:

Teacher: _____ Date benchmark assessment completed: _____

Level 27

Reading Record

Name: _____ **Age:** _____ **Date:** _____

Text: _Preparing for a Day in the Forest_ **Level:** 27 **R. W:** 217

Text type: _Procedural_ **Accuracy:** _____ **S.C. Rate:** _____

This nonfiction text explains how to prepare for a day of hiking in the forest.	E	S.C.	Errors MSV	Self corrections MSV
Exploring hills and forests can be exciting. But it is very important to be well prepared for any emergency. You will need to decide where you are going and who will accompany you. Always go with an adult. You should never explore forests alone. Be sure to wear suitable clothing. Many people wear long pants and socks to protect their legs from insect bites and scratches from the undergrowth. It is a good idea to wear a loose shirt with long sleeves that can be rolled up. Comfortable shoes or walking boots are essential. You will need a sunhat, too. Take a sturdy backpack. The best packs have useful pockets on the outside. Put a waterproof jacket, a warm sweater, and an extra pair of socks in your pack, just in case the weather changes. Pack a plastic lunch box with fruit, vegetables, nuts, and sandwiches that you can eat during the day. Snacks such as cookies and chocolate bars will help to give you energy. Take a large bottle of water to prevent dehydration. The adult with you should take a cell phone and a small first-aid kit. Don't forget the sunscreen. Before you leave, check the weather forecast. Last of all, remember to tell someone where you are going and when you expect to return.				
Total				

Reading Record © Rigby, 2002.
This page may be photocopied for educational use within the purchasing institution.

Level 27: *Preparing for a Day in the Forest*

Assessment Record

Name: _____

Analysis of retelling *(meaning, main ideas, coherence, vocabulary, reference to text)*

_____

_____

Questions to check for understanding *(check if understanding acceptable)*

1. Why is it sensible to wear long pants and socks when you are walking through undergrowth? ☐
   Response: (to protect your legs from insect bites and scratches)

2. Why should you pack a warm sweater and an extra pair of socks when you go exploring hills and forests? ☐
   Response: (in case the weather turns cold or your feet get wet)

3. What does dehydration mean? ☐
   Response: (the body loses water)

4. Why do you think it is a good idea to tell someone where you are going and when you expect to return? Why not just rely on a cell phone? ☐
   Response: (a cell phone could get lost or broken)

5. Describe an emergency that could happen when you are out in the forest for a day. ☐
   Response: (answers will vary)

Reading level

Accuracy level: $\dfrac{217-\_\_\_\_}{217}$ = _____ %

Self-correction rate: _____ = _____ = 1: _____

Reading level *(with understanding):* Easy / Instructional / Hard

Analysis of reading behaviors *(print concepts, meaning cues, structural cues, visual information, self-monitoring, self-correcting, fluency, expression)*

Recommendations: _____

Teacher: _____ **Date benchmark assessment completed:** _____

Level 28

Reading Record

Name: _____	Age: _____	Date: _____
Text: Tracks by the Stream	Level: 28	R. W: 213
	Accuracy: _____	S.C. Rate: _____

This piece is about some pioneers named Jo, Jim, and Ben who are traveling west in a covered wagon.	E	S.C.	Errors MSV	Self corrections MSV
After a thousand miles, the trail left the treeless plains. It led the pioneers ever westward into mountains clad in pine forests. They feasted their eyes on range after range of snow-capped peaks. This change was a great relief after the scorching heat of the plains. At the end of each day on the trail, Jo and Jim and their brother Ben camped near running water. There were trout in the streams, so whenever there was an opportunity, they rushed to try their luck. Fresh fish were welcome because their food supplies were dwindling. September had come, and the nights, cool with the first touch of autumn, were made colder by the winds blowing down from the high snowfields. The family sat near the fire for warmth, and shivered under their blankets in the wagon at night. One evening, as they were collecting pine cones as fuel for the fire, Jo discovered something odd. She came rushing back to Ben, breathless with excitement. "I've found some strange tracks, like giant's feet, down there by the stream," she gasped. Ben left the oxen and the wagon, and ran with Jo to the stream. He whistled when he saw the huge paw prints in the damp ground. "A grizzly!" he exclaimed. "Those are bear tracks."				
Total				

74

Reading Record © Rigby, 2002.
This page may be photocopied for educational use within the purchasing institution.

Level 28: *Tracks by the Stream*

Assessment Record

Name: _____

Analysis of retelling *(meaning, main ideas, coherence, vocabulary, reference to text)*

_____

Questions to check for understanding *(check if understanding acceptable)*

1. What made the winds so cold when the pioneers reached the mountains? ☐
   Response: (they were blowing down from the high snowfields)

2. In this story, what did the pioneers use as fuel for their fires? ☐
   Response: (pine cones)

3. What made the strange tracks by the stream? ☐
   Response: (a grizzly bear)

4. What do you think the author meant when she said, "They feasted their eyes on range after range of snow-capped peaks?" ☐
   Response: (They had probably never seen mountains before and were captivated them)

5. How do you know that this is not a modern story? Explain some of the details that are different from life today. ☐
   Response: (oxen and wagon, pioneers, fire, travel westward, etc.)

Reading level

Accuracy level: $\dfrac{213-}{213}$ = _____ %

Self-correction rate: _____ = _____ = 1:

Reading level *(with understanding):*   Easy / Instructional / Hard

Analysis of reading behaviors *(print concepts, meaning cues, structural cues, visual information, self-monitoring, self-correcting, fluency, expression)*

Recommendations:

Teacher: _____   Date benchmark assessment completed: _____

Level 29

Reading Record

Name: _____ Age: _____ Date: _____

Text: _Cyclone Tracy Destroys Darwin_ Level: _29_ R. W: _209_

Text type: _Report_ Accuracy: _____ S.C. Rate: _____

This nonfiction text is written as a newspaper account of what happened when Cyclone Tracy hit the city of Darwin.	E	S.C.	Errors MSV	Self corrections MSV
The city of Darwin, Australia, was devastated early on Wednesday, December 25, by Cyclone Tracy. At least 40 people are known to be dead, and hundreds are badly injured. Ninety-five per cent of the city's buildings have been damaged by winds that reached speeds of 125 miles an hour. It is thought that 20,000 people are homeless. Most of Darwin's houses have lost roofs and walls, and many look like crushed matchboxes. The streets are littered with damaged cars and building materials such as glass and iron. Electric cables and phone lines are down, and water pipes have been torn away. A man using a radio transmitter reported, "Darwin looks as though it has been hit by an atom bomb." The hospital has no roof. The airport buildings have been destroyed, and parked aircraft are a mass of twisted metal. Many boats have been tossed ashore, and at least four fishing boats are missing. Warning sirens had been blaring every 15 minutes since noon on Tuesday. Sergeant Taylor of the Darwin police said, "There was little that anyone could do. You can't hold your roof on." Many people tried to find shelter in bathrooms and basements, under beds, or inside closets. When Cyclone Tracy struck at about 1 a.m., the winds were blowing from the northeast.				
Allow student to finish reading the text. **Total**				

Level 29: *Cyclone Tracy Destroys Darwin*

Assessment Record

Name: _____

Analysis of retelling *(meaning, main ideas, coherence, vocabulary, reference to text)*

_____

_____

Questions to check for understanding *(check if understanding acceptable)*

1. What caused all the damage when this cyclone struck Darwin? ☐
   Response: (winds that reached speeds of 125 mph)

2. After the electric cables and telephone lines were broken, how was information about the cyclone sent from Darwin? ☐
   Response: (a radio transmitter)

3. Where did many people try to find shelter? ☐
   Response: (bathrooms, basements, under beds, closets)

4. Why do you think the city had to be evacuated? ☐
   Response: (answers will vary but should include safety concerns)

5. Explain what is meant by *the eye of the storm*. ☐
   Response: (an area in the center where winds are calm)

Reading level

Accuracy level: $\dfrac{209-}{209} = $ %

Self-correction rate: _____ = _____ = 1:

Reading level *(with understanding):*   Easy / Instructional / Hard

Analysis of reading behaviors *(print concepts, meaning cues, structural cues, visual information, self-monitoring, self-correcting, fluency, expression)*

_____

_____

Recommendations:

Teacher: _____   Date benchmark assessment completed: _____

Level 30

Reading Record

Name: _____ Age: _____ Date: _____

Text: __Black Beauty Encounters a Steam Train__ Level: __30__ R. W: __229__

Accuracy: _____ S.C. Rate: _____

This piece is from the book *Black Beauty* and takes place when the horse is being trained.	E	S.C.	Errors MSV	Self corrections MSV
As one part of my training, my master sent me to a neighboring farm. I was put in a meadow, which was skirted by a railway line. I shall never forget the first steam train that ran by. I was feeding quietly by the fence when I heard an extraordinary sound in the distance. Before I knew where it was coming from — with a rush and a clatter and a great deal of smoke — a long black object thundered by. I turned and galloped frantically to the far side of the meadow, and there I stood snorting with astonishment and fear. In the course of the day, many of these long black objects drew up at the station close by. Sometimes they made a ghastly shriek and groan before they stopped. I thought them most alarming, but the cows calmly went on eating. They hardly raised their heads as the monstrous objects came puffing and grinding past. For the first few days I could not feed in peace, but as I found that these terrible creatures never came into the field, nor did me any harm, I began to disregard them. Since then I have seen many horses panic-stricken at the sight or sound of a steam train — but thanks to my master's careful training, I am as fearless at railway stations as I am in my own stable.				
Total				

Level 30: *Black Beauty Encounters a Steam Train*

Assessment Record

Name: _____

Analysis of retelling *(meaning, main ideas, coherence, vocabulary, reference to text)*

_____

_____

Questions to check for understanding *(check if understanding acceptable)*

1. This story uses the words *I* and *me*. Who is telling the story? ☐
   Response: (the horse Black Beauty)

2. What was part of the careful training Black Beauty's master gave him? ☐
   Response: (keeping the horse in a field by a railway line)

3. What does "skirted by a railway line" mean? ☐
   Response: (railroad tracks went around it)

4. What do you think the author's feelings are about horses? ☐
   Response: (answers will vary but should be positive)

5. Explain why a horse that is terrified of trains would be a danger to itself and its rider. ☐
   Response: (the horse could bolt or throw its rider)

Reading level

Accuracy level: $\dfrac{229-}{229}$ = _____ %

Self-correction rate: _____ = _____ = 1:

Reading level *(with understanding):*   Easy / Instructional / Hard

Analysis of reading behaviors *(print concepts, meaning cues, structural cues, visual information, self-monitoring, self-correcting, fluency, expression)*

_____

_____

Recommendations:

Teacher: _____   Date benchmark assessment completed: _____

Record of Reading Progress

Name: *John SMITH* **D.O.B.** _5/12/1996_

Level	Reading Age				
Level 30					
Level 29					
Level 28					
Level 27					4/28
Level 26					
Level 25					2/3
Level 24					
Level 23					9/18
Level 22					5/7
Level 21					
Level 20				11/20	
Level 19					
Level 18				9/8	
Level 17				5/10	
Level 16				2/13	
Level 15			12/13		
Level 14					
Level 13			10/13		
Level 12			4/30		
Level 11					
Level 10		3/11			
Level 9					
Level 8		1/15			
Level 7					
Level 6					
Level 5		10/20			
Level 4					
Level 3					
Level 2	9/12				
Level 1					
Class Level	Grade 1	Grade 2	Grade 3	Grade 4	Grade 5
Year	2002-03	2003-04	2004-05	2005-06	2006-07
Schools	Hilltop	Hilltop	Hilltop	Hilltop	Hilltop

- More than one assessment may be recorded within each year.

Reading Progress Record © Rigby, 2002.
This page may be photocopied for educational use within the purchasing institution.

Record of Reading Progress

Name: _____ D.O.B. _____

Level	Reading Age				
Level 30					
Level 29					
Level 28					
Level 27					
Level 26					
Level 25					
Level 24					
Level 23					
Level 22					
Level 21					
Level 20					
Level 19					
Level 18					
Level 17					
Level 16					
Level 15					
Level 14					
Level 13					
Level 12					
Level 11					
Level 10					
Level 9					
Level 8					
Level 7					
Level 6					
Level 5					
Level 4					
Level 3					
Level 2					
Level 1					
Class Level					
Year					
School/s					

- More than one assessment may be recorded within each year.

Reading Progress Record © Rigby, 2002
This page may be photocopied for educational use within the purchasing institution.

Reading Record

Level ___

Name: _____ **Age:** _____ **Date:** _____

Text: _____ **Level:** _____ **R. W:** _____

Accuracy: _____ **S.C. Rate:** _____

Page		E	S.C.	Errors MSV	Self corrections MSV
	Total				

Accuracy Level Chart

(Match the number of errors to the corresponding accuracy level percentage.)

Level 1 – *On the table* — Running Words 56

%	98	96	94	92	91	89	87	85	83	82	80	78	76	75	73
Errors	1	2	3	4	5	6	7	8	9	10	11	12	13	14	15

Level 2 – *At the zoo* — Running Words 43

%	97	95	93	90	88	86	83	81	79	76	74	72	69	67	65
Errors	1	2	3	4	5	6	7	8	9	10	11	12	13	14	15

Level 3 – *Kate goes to a farm* — Running Words 69

%	99	97	96	94	93	91	90	88	87	86	84	83	81	80	78
Errors	1	2	3	4	5	6	7	8	9	10	11	12	13	14	15

Level 4 – *The big plane* — Running Words 83

%	98	97	96	95	94	92	91	90	89	88	86	85	84	83	82
Errors	1	2	3	4	5	6	7	8	9	10	11	12	13	14	15

Level 5 – *Little Teddy helps Mouse* — Running Words 91

%	98	97	96	95	94	93	92	91	90	89	87	86	85	84	83
Errors	1	2	3	4	5	6	7	8	9	10	11	12	13	14	15

Level 6 – *Nick's snowman* — Running Words 104
Level 7 – *Baby Bear and the big fish* — Running Words 100

%	99	98	97	96	95	94	93	92	91	90	89	88	87	86	85
Errors	1	2	3	4	5	6	7	8	9	10	11	12	13	14	15

%	84	83	82	81	80	79	78	77	76	75	74	73	72	71	70
Errors	16	17	18	19	20	21	22	23	24	25	26	27	28	29	30

Level 8 – *My big sister* — Running Words 110

%	99	98	97	96	95	94	93	92	91	90	89	88	87	86	85
Errors	1	2	3	4	5	6	7	8	9	10-11	12	13	14	15	16

Level 9 – *Clever Little Dinosaur* — Running Words 107

%	99	98	97	96	95	94	93	92	91	90	89	88	87	86	85
Errors	1	2	3	4	5	6	7	8	9	10	11	12	13	14	15

Level 10 – *The helpful bulldozer* — Running Words 116

%	99	98	97	96	95	94	93	92	91	90	89	88	87	86	85
Errors	1	2	3	4	5	6	7-8	9	10	11	12	13	14-15	16	17

Level 11 – *Tom's train ride* — Running Words 120
Level 12 – *Buying a new house* — Running Words 121

%	99	98	97	96	95	94	93	92	91	90	89	88	87	86	85
Errors	1	2	3	4	5-6	7	8	9	10	11-12	13	14	15	16	17-18

%	84	83	82	81	80	79	78	77	76	75	74	73	72	71	70
Errors	19	20	21	22	23-24	25	26	27	28	29-30	31	32	33	34	35-36

Level 13 – *The best runner* (see Levels 16 and 17 also) — Running Words 133

%	99	98	97	96	95	94	93	92	91	90	89	88	87	86	85
Errors	1	2	3	4-5	6	7	8-9	10	11	12-13	14	15	16-17	18	19

Level 14 – *Little Hen, Mouse, and Rabbit* — Running Words 140

%	99	98	97	96	95	94	93	92	91	90	89	88	87	86	85
Errors	1	2	3-4	5	6-7	8	9	10-11	12	13-14	15	16	17-18	19	20

Level 15 – *Skip Goes to the Rescue* — Running Words 135

%	99	98	97	96	95	94	93	92	91	90	89	88	87	86	85
Errors	1	2	3-4	5	6	7-8	9	10	11-12	13	14	15-16	17	18	19-20

Level 16 – *The Classroom Play* — Running Words 132
Level 17 – *The Greedy Dog and the Bone* — Running Words 133

%	99	98	97	96	95	94	93	92	91	90	89	88	87	86
Errors	1	2	3	4-5	6	7	8-9	10	11	12-13	14	15	16-17	18

%	85	84	83	82	81	80	79	78	77	76	75	74
Errors	19	20-21	22	23	24-25	26	27	28-29	30	31	32–33	34

Level 18 – *Harvest Mice* — Running Words 138

%	99	98	97	96	95	94	93	92	91	90	89	88	87	86
Errors	1	2	3-4	5	6	7-8	9	10-11	12	13	14-15	16	17	18-19

Level 19 – *The Old Cabin in the Forest* — Running Words 143

%	99	98	97	96	95	94	93	92	91	90	89	88	87	86
Errors	1	2	3-4	5	6-7	8	9-10	11	12	13-14	15	16-17	18	19

Level 20 – *Leo the Lion Cub* — Running Words 153

%	99	98	97	96	95	94	93	92	91	90	89	88	87	86	86
Errors	1-2	3	4-5	6	7-8	9	10-11	12	13	14-15	16	17-18	19	20-21	22

Level 21 – *Kwan the Artist* — Running Words 204
Level 22 – *Trees on Our Planet* — Running Words 207

%	99	98	97	96	95	94	93	92
Errors	1-2	3-4	5-6	7-8	9-10	11-12	13-14	15-16

%	91	90	89	88	87	86	85	84	
Errors	17-18	19-20	21-22	23-24	25-26	27-28	29-30	31-32	

Level 23 – *The Miller, His Son, and Their Donkey* — Running Words 209
Level 24 – *A New Skatepark* — Running Words 209

%	99	98	97	96	95	94	93	92
Errors	1-2	3-4	5-6	7-8	9-10	11-12	13-14	15-16

%	91	90	89	88	87	86	85	84
Errors	17-18	19-20	21-22	23-25	26-27	28-29	30-31	32-33

Level 25 – *Beavers* Running Words 200

%	99	98	97	96	95	94	93	92
Errors	1- 2	3 – 4	5 - 6	7 - 8	9 - 10	11 - 12	13 - 14	15-16

%	91	90	89	88	87	86	85	84
Errors	17- 18	19 – 20	21 - 22	23 - 24	25 - 26	27 - 28	29- 30	31-32

Level 26 – *A Great Sense of Smell* Running Words 209

%	99	98	97	96	95	94	93	92
Errors	1- 2	3 – 4	5 - 6	7 - 8	9 - 10	11 - 12	13 - 14	15-16

%	91	90	89	88	87	86	85	84
Errors	17- 18	19 – 20	21 - 22	23 - 25	26 - 27	28 - 29	30- 31	32-33

Level 27 – *Preparing for a Day in the Forest* Running Words 217
Level 28 – *Tracks by the Stream* Running Words 213

%	99	98	97	96	95	94	93	92
Errors	1- 2	3 – 4	5 - 6	7 - 8	9 - 10	11 - 12	13 - 14	15-17

%	91	90	89	88	87	86	85	84
Errors	18- 19	20 – 21	22 - 23	24 - 25	26 - 27	28 - 29	30- 31	32-35

Level 29 – *Cyclone Tracy Destroys Darwin* Running Words 209

%	99	98	97	96	95	94	93	92
Errors	1- 2	3 – 4	5 - 6	7 - 8	9 - 10	11 - 12	13 - 14	15-16

%	91	90	89	88	87	86	85	84
Errors	17- 18	19 – 20	21 - 22	23 - 25	26 - 27	28 - 29	30- 31	32-33

Level 30 – *Black Beauty Encounters a Steam Train* Running Words 229

%	99	98	97	96	95	94	93	92
Errors	1- 2	3 – 4	5 - 6	7 - 9	10 - 11	12 - 13	14 - 16	17 - 18

%	91	90	89	88	87	86	85	84
Errors	19 - 20	21 – 22	23 - 25	26 - 27	28 - 29	30 - 32	33 - 34	35 -36

Teacher's Notes

Teacher's Notes